Airborne Free

Airborne Free

Red Devils and Other Rare Breeds

Cartoons for
**The Airborne Forces Charities Development
Trust**
and
The David Shepherd Conservation Foundation

EDITED BY MARK BRYANT

Leo Cooper
London

First published 1990 by Leo Cooper

Leo Cooper is an independent imprint of the
Octopus Publishing Group, Michelin House,
81 Fulham Road, London SW3 6RB

LONDON MELBOURNE AUCKLAND

Cartoons copyright © 1989 the artists

A CIP catalogue record for this book
is available from the British Library
ISBN 0–85052–152X

Printed in Great Britain by
Richard Clay Ltd, Bungay, Suffolk

About This Book

1990 is the fiftieth anniversary of the foundation of Airborne Forces – a division of the British Army that originally included the Parachute Regiment and battalions or units of other regiments, services and corps, and the SAS and Glider Pilots regiments. It also marks thirty years of work dedicated to wildlife conservation by the renowned artist, David Shepherd OBE, FRSA, whose first painting of elephants was commissioned by the Royal Air Force in Kenya when he was employed as an aviation artist. Thus it seemed appropriate that, to tie in with the Airborne Forces Anniversary 'PARA 90' and The David Shepherd Conservation Foundation's own activities, the occasion should be celebrated by a cartoon book, exhibition and auction embracing these twin themes, and introduced by H.R.H. The Prince of Wales – Colonel-in-Chief of the Parachute Regiment and Patron of the Airborne Forces Charities Development Trust and himself a keen conservationist – whose sense of humour has endeared him to millions.

All royalties from sales of this book and all proceeds of the auction go to The Airborne Forces Charities Development Trust and The David Shepherd Conservation Foundation for Wildlife and the Environment.

Thanks are due to all those cartoonists whose generosity has made this book and the auction possible and to the editors of the various newspapers and magazines in which some of the cartoons first appeared. Special thanks also go to Lieutenant-General Sir Michael Gray KCB, OBE, Colonel David Mallam OBE and Jane Riddell of the Airborne Forces Charities Development Trust; David Shepherd OBE, FRSA, and Michael Zilka of The David Shepherd Conservation Foundation; to Leo Cooper, Beryl Hill and Tom Hartman for all their help.

M.B.

Acknowledgements

For their kind permission to use the cartoons
in this book, the charities and the publishers
would like to thank the following:

Evening Standard
The Independent
Knight Features
Mail Newspapers
Mirror Group Newspapers
News Group Newspapers
Private Eye
Punch
The Spectator

Also Stella Gibbons and Curtis Brown Ltd for
the use of 'The Giraffes' by Stella Gibbons
from *Collected Poems* (London, 1950).

The Giraffes

I saw, between a page's turning,
Shapes on the distant desert burning.
Shadows running, swift and far,
Where the white clouds of morning are.

It was the herds of gold giraffes
That couple with the hippogriffes,
And run with tireless shoulders bare
To the more golden desert air:
The joyous herds that feed on leaves
The sun from hidden rhizome weaves,
And bathe with great, strong-striding flanks
Where hidden waters press their banks:
The herds that sleep not through the night
But fly through miles of cool blue light
Circling never nearer than
Seven long leagues in sight of Man:
The gentle herds that die unseen
In Chi's stone vale of age-carved green
And whose delight is still to run
Like wind between the sands and sun.

I hid the doubt that suddenly
Troubled my mind's tranquillity.
'What if those golden beasts should find
The secret out before mankind?
And if their draught of movement's wine
Teach them before these books of mine?
If they are nearer to the True
Than Wisdom?' pierced doubt's arrow through.

Stella Gibbons

Foreword

In 1940, the first Airborne units were formed following a Minute to the Chiefs of Staff on 22 June from Sir Winston Churchill that 'We ought to have a Corps of at least 5,000 parachute troops.' Now, in 1990, we are celebrating the fiftieth anniversary of Airborne Forces.

But quite apart from the planned celebrations for 1990, there is a fast-growing need to increase the endowment fund which looks after the financial requirements of those in need or distress who have served in Airborne Forces. This fund has cared for members and their families since it was set up in 1942. The 1990s will bring its greatest task so far, to help the tens of thousands who served in The Second World War who are now entering their seventies and eighties.

It is also splendid that this fund should be associated with the work of David Shepherd, who has personally raised well over a million pounds for wildlife and other charities. He has formed a charitable foundation to act as its own 'rapid intervention force' to support wildlife and conservation projects. And this appeal is to support that Foundation too.

I am very pleased to have been asked to write the Foreword to this amusing and worthwhile charity cartoon book, which will bring a lot of pleasure to those who support both the Airborne Forces charities and The David Shepherd Conservation Foundation.

'He's very upset, he landed on an ant.'

'That white rhino is a menace – he's determined not to become
extinct!'

I don't know about you, but personally I'm getting just a little fed up with all this posing for David Shepherd !

'Someone should have a word with Tucker . . . everything by the book.'

'Very clever, but if those 'chutes don't open, it won't do much for conservation . . .!'

'Coming over? – We've got regurgitated squid tonight!'

'You won't be needing this, lad. The idea is for you to sort of . . .
hop down!'

N
W E
S
I THINK
THERE'S SOMETHING
WRONG WITH THIS
ALTIMETER, SARGE!

CAUTION!
YOU ARE NOW IN
A
FLORA + FAUNA
CONSERVATION
AREA
CARELESS FEET
COST
LIVES!
CLIVE COLLINS

'For the last time . . . David Attenborough isn't here . . . now get
rid of the eye make-up!'

'I said members of the Parachute Regiment free-fall display team
are a pain in the arse at parties!'

OKAY, PARATROOPS — JUMP!
BUT WE'VE NO PARACHUTES, SERGE
© Harry Hargreaves, 1972

THE PARAS ARE THE TOUGHEST TROOPS IN THE ARMY — RIGHT?
RIGHT!

OKAY, PARATROOPS — JUMP!
HARGREAVES

'Rare? Yes, it was rare – so rare that it's now extinct.'

THE PARACHUTE REGIMENT
FREE FALL
DEMONSTRATION
TEAM

'It's not the jump we object to – it's the positioning of the
doorway!'

'Be seeing you – man willing.'

'It's my second week.'

'. . . You know, out of all the animal species, I reckon the human
must be about the nearest to us in intelligence.'

'Another damn package tour from Gadarene!'

'Give over, Pritchard – we've all seen your Marilyn Monroe
impression!'

'Uncle Herbert was really pleased that David Shepherd could
arrange for him to do the charity parachute jump.'

'Aw, for Heaven's sake, Leo – she was only trying to help!'

Shower Gel
Soap
LES BARTON

'Black rhino – fortunately for us, they're very nearly extinct!'

Simon Bond

SAVE
THE
DODO

PARACHUTE REGIMENT FREE FALL BAND

WOODCOCK

'You'll never get away with it!'

'. . . the 10th Duke at Mafeking, the 11th on the Somme, the 12th at Alamein, and Pater watching *Wogan* with a takeaway TV dinner!'

'At ease, men – it's only David Shepherd dropping in his latest
commission!'

'Over and over I say "Stop water pollution *now*" – but I'm never
sure whether he grasps it.'

'You've certainly got them well drilled!'

'You shouldn't have allowed him to jump. He's an endangered species.'

'Sorry – I didn't know you had company.'

'Look upon me as you would your fathers.'

'No, no, Julian – what I actually said was go in and capture the
leader of the *guerrilla* band.'

'I'll go for help. And whatever you do, David, don't stop
painting.'

'Hello! John Nott's been shopping in Soho!'

'It may be quicker, Thompson, but it's upsetting the visitors.'

'Does your mother never give up, Aitchison?!'

Cluff

'Ten years ago Tarzan would have made that jump without a
'chute!'

MR. TIGGY-
-WINKLE

SUPPORT FOR SANCTIONS. AGAINST S.A.
Garland

'We'll drop you through the hole in the ozone layer!'

'Ye gods! Yetis are into self-abuse!'

'Is Private Wilson supposed to be part of the picture, major?'

(Cartoon version of *Winter of '43* by David Shepherd. *Ed.*)

'I used to be influenced by David Shepherd. Now I lean more
towards David Hockney.'

FASTER! DAMMIT, FASTER!
TORY RIGHT
ALL POSSIBLE COMPROMISE
INVASION

I HAVE BEEN TO THE SAFARI PARK
WE HAVE BEEN TO THE SAFARI PARK
WE HAVE BEEN TO THE SAFARI PARK
STOWELL

'Get back, copper, or I'll blast a hole in the ozone layer.'

'Sounds like they've got a rhin . . .'

'Sounds like they've got a rhin . . .'

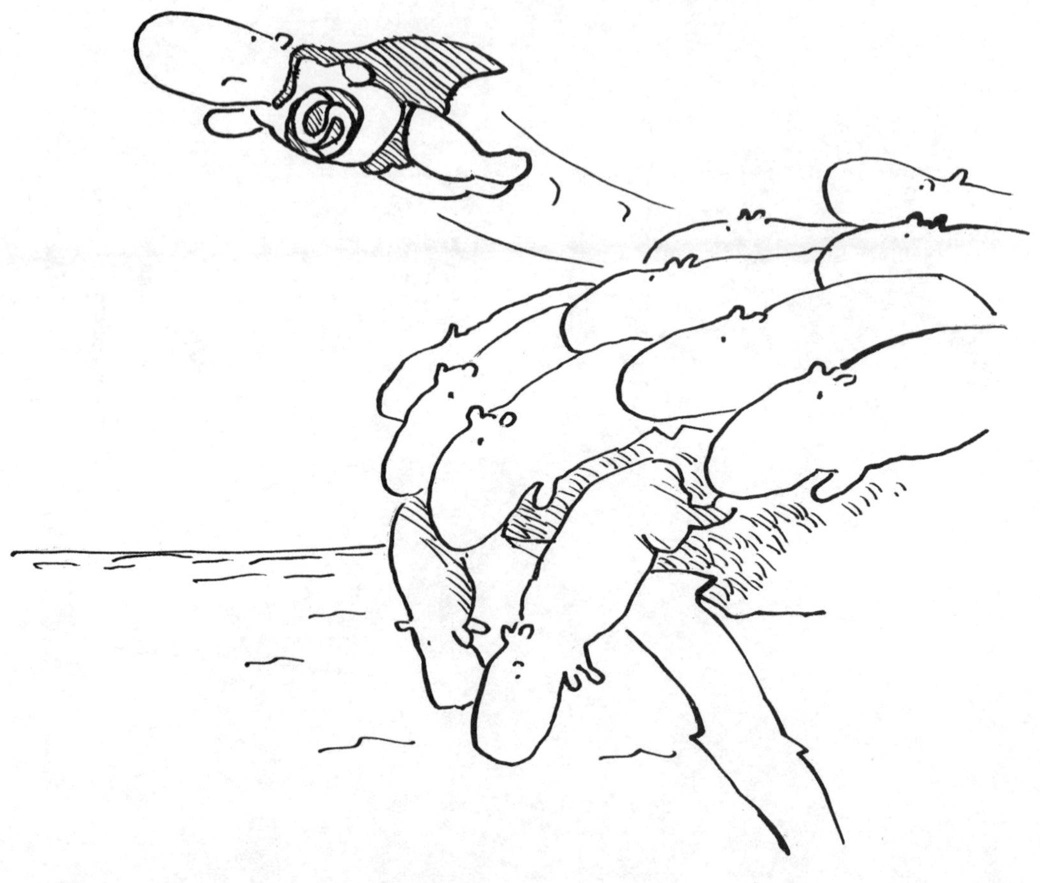

IT ISN'T —!!!!
IT CAN'T BE —!!
PRUE FORREST!!

'Anne presses flowers; Charlotte presses flowers. Why can't you
press flowers, Emily?'

FRED BASSET
by GRAHAM

CYANIDE
POISON
help!
NOW RUN
ALONG AND PLAY.

'Bloody defence cuts!'

'I like to come here to unwind.'

'His parachute didn't open and now he's scared stiff of heights.'

THAT HAWK'S AN
ENDANGERED SPECIES

NO WONDER!

'Whaling ship sighted – harpoon gun ready . . .'

'That man's improperly dressed, sergeant. He should have leaves
on at this time of year.'

'What do you mean, "It's a bird"? I thought it was a missile.'

'OK. If not for me, for them.'

WELCOME TO
WINDSOR
SAFARI PARK
—
PLEASE KEEP
YOUR WINDOWS
SHUT
THESE ANIMALS BITE
Roy Nixon

'Personally, I preferred pollution.'

CARLING
BLACK
LABEL

'How staggering to think that all this grew from one tiny acorn.'

ART
GECKO
CATALOGUE
Cluff

'Guess what! We're now appearing in fish fingers – anonymously,
of course.'

Gibbard
AIRBORNE FORCES RESCUE

'I'll be honest, men . . . there'd have been more chance of a successful escape had we managed to finish the tunnel *before* Christmas.'

'And that's Great-great Uncle Titus. Bit of an embarrassment, really
— he shot the very last dodo.'

'I don't care if the SAS *did* dress as sheep in the Falklands – take
them off!'

'Don't shoot! Here, take them!'

'Well – can you see any ivory poachers?'

'They tell me it's not even safe to drink the water.'

'The trick is to get south before icicles hang by the wall and Dick
the shepherd blows his nail, and Tom bears logs into the hall . . .'

D
INDUSTRIAL RELATIONS ACT
MARGARET THATCHER
HAROLD WILSON
EDWARD HEATH

'What is a chicken, anyway?'

'I think he's new to this game!'

'Dear Mum and Dad . . . At last I'm amongst friends . . .'

'Our bravest man, he plays reveille every morning.'

'That, I'm afraid, sir, is a private nightingale, and it will cost you
£2 to be half in love with easeful Death.'

MILITARY SHOW JUMPING
MILITARY   MPING

'OK – so where's John Wayne?'

KEVIN
WOODCOCK

'I don't think the public are ready for German Shepherds down the
trousers, constable . . .'

'And another thing, I don't like them calling it a "terminal".'

'Wildlife's not what it used to be, Bosworth.'

'I'm beginning to wonder if the nose-job was such a good idea . . .'

'And this was "Taxidermy" Thompson's very last piece . . .'

'This is quite remarkable. It seems the female is knitting me a
cardigan.'

'Paras never seem to get the hang of it.'

Index of Cartoons

Contributing Cartoonists

GEORGE ADAMSON

A US citizen but a British subject, George Adamson was a Catalina flying-boat navigator for Coastal Command in the war years and an official war artist when his duties allowed. He became a fellow of the Royal Society of Painter-Etchers and Engravers in 1987 and has exhibited at the Royal Academy. There are also collections of his work in the British Museum, V&A, New York Public Library and elsewhere. A humorist and regular contributor to *Punch*, he has also illustrated a number of books, including the first five volumes of *Private Eye*'s 'Dear Bill' series and a collection of P. G. Wodehouse short stories for the Folio Society.

'ALBERT' – ALBERT RUSLING   b1944

Albert Rusling left school at 15 and spent nine years in an advertising agency before becoming a full-time cartoonist in 1968. He has written and illustrated a number of books and contributed cartoons to many national and regional publications including *Punch, Private Eye, Guardian* and *Financial Times*. He now lives in Cheshire and works to support one wife, two children, two collie dogs, one gerbil, one house and a partridge in a pear tree.

KEN ALLEN

Ken Allen is 28 years old and lives in Liverpool. He sold his first cartoon to the *Liverpool Weekly News* in 1987 and now draws a daily pocket cartoon for the *Liverpool Daily Post*. His ambition is to watch Southport Football Club win something.

SALLY ARTZ   b1935

Born in London, Sally Artz sold her first cartoon in 1955 and has since contributed to a wide variety of publications, including *Punch, Reader's Digest* and *Penthouse* (USA), plus long-running features in the *Daily Mirror* and the *People*. She has also worked in book illustration, advertising and cartoon animation, is married with three children and now lives in Bath.

NICK BAKER

A freelance cartoonist since 1971, Nick Baker is a regular contributor to *Punch, Private Eye, Financial Times, Daily Mirror, Daily Express* etc and also draws for advertising/publicity. He has written three children's books featuring 'The One-Eyed Lion' and 'Graham the Gorilla' and has produced two volumes of captionless cartoons, *Bad Manners* and *Bad Losers*. He enjoys travel and 'on the spot' drawing events.

LES BARTON   b1923

Born in Dorset, Les Barton now lives in Uxbridge, Middlesex. He started life as an airbrush artist in an advertising studio and drew pin-up cartoons at a time when posing in swimming costumes was considered naughty. After a period drawing for comics like *I Spy* and *Billy Bunter*, he now contributes regularly to *Punch, Private Eye* and *Truth* and various overseas publications. His greetings cards of amorphous animals also keep him busy. He is Honorary Treasurer of the Cartoonists' Club of Great Britain and his hobbies include watching Arsenal FC.

NEIL BENNETT

Neil Bennett became a full-time cartoonist at the age of 46, having resigned from teaching English in a college of further education. He contributes to *Private Eye, Punch, New Statesman* and *The Cricketer*.

SIMON BOND b1947

A course at the West Sussex College of Art and Design led to eight months on the dole before Simon found work in Nottingham as a paste-up artist on the *Tatler*, only to be sacked for illness. After a period as manager of a jewellery shop he took advantage of his dual citizenship to emigrate to America in 1970, settling in Phoenix, Arizona, and drawing cartoons for a number of magazines. The publication, in 1981, of *101 Uses for A Dead Cat* brought him worldwide success and notoriety. Since then he has produced a number of books, some of them funny.

'CHAS' – CHAS SINCLAIR

Chas Sinclair left school at 14 and began work in the aircraft industry before leaving to draw editorial cartoons for the *TV Post*. After a period working as designer for a linen manufacturers he was made redundant in 1967 and has been a freelance cartoonist ever since, contributing to the *Mail on Sunday, Shoot!* etc.

'CHIC' – CHIC JACOB b1926

Born in Dulwich, Chic Jacob received no art training – 'too much of a luxury in wartime Britain' – but had plenty of experience on farms (as an evacuee in Sussex) and service in the Royal Navy before the war ended. He is a regular contributor to *Punch, Observer, Law Society Gazette* and other less posh publications.

'CLUFF' – JOHN LONGSTAFF b1949

After a graphics course, 'Cluff' worked in local government. He began cartooning eight years ago and is now printed in *Private Eye, Punch* and *Literary Review*. When not working or busy bringing up his six-year-old daughter he enjoys walking in the Yorkshire Dales.

CLIVE COLLINS b1942

Went to Kingston Art School, after which he worked in insurance, as a film extra, ran a film studio and repped for a small artwork studio, before becoming political cartoonist for the *Sunday People*. He is now deputy political cartoonist on the *Daily Mirror*, and regularly draws cartoons for *Punch* and *Playboy*. He was selected as Cartoonist of the Year by the Cartoonists' Club of Great Britain in 1984, 1985 and 1987, and was President of the Salon Jury, to mention just a few of the accolades he has been awarded over the years.

DEREK CROWTER

Derek Crowter joined the Royal Marines in 1953 when he was 18 and served as a Royal Orderly – the offical guard to the Royal Family – on the Royal Yacht *Britannia* between 1959 and 1965. After a year working on the *Portsmouth News* he joined the Royal Navy and later became Security Petty Officer on the *QE2*. His cartoons have appeared in every national newspaper in the UK as well as many magazines and trade publications.

MIKE DARLING

Mike Darling served as a pilot in the RAF and studied painting and drawing at the Harrow School of Art and the Royal Academy Schools. He is a regular contributor to *Punch* and other publications, has taught drawing and lectured on the history of art at various colleges, and has exhibited many of his own paintings.

PETE DREDGE b1952

Born in Nottingham, Pete Dredge has been a professional cartoonist since 1976 and is a regular contributor to *Punch, Private Eye, Listener, Spectator, Radio Times* and *Daily Express*. He was voted Joke Cartoonist of the Year 1986 and Provincial Press Cartoonist of the Year 1987 by the Cartoonists' Club of Great Britain.

PATRICIA DRENNAN

Pat Drennan is 55 and studied art in Belfast and Palermo before teaching in London. Currently specializing in advertising and book illustration, she has had cartoons published in *Punch, Reader's*

Digest and many national newspapers and magazines as well as professional journals etc. She is married with three children and lives in Hampshire.

BARRY FANTONI b1940

A novelist, broadcaster, cartoonist and jazz musician. Has been on the editorial staff of *Private Eye* since 1963 and diary cartoonist of *The Times* since 1983. Studied at Camberwell School of Arts and Crafts. Has cartooned for *The Listener*, been art critic of *The Times* and has been a film and TV actor. His recreations are snooker, road running and animal welfare.

NOEL FORD b1942

Having survived a direct hit on his pram by the RAF (they were dropping practice firecrackers at the time), Noel Ford was educated at King Edward VI Grammar School, Nuneaton, and Birmingham College of Arts and Crafts. He then played lead guitar in a travelling band (gave up after appearing on New Faces!) and dabbled in short-story writing for magazines and BBC radio before becoming a full-time cartoonist. He has contributed to *Punch* for twelve years, is deputy editorial cartoonist on the *Daily Star* and his work has appeared in *Private Eye* and many other newspapers and magazines. He also draws cartoons for greetings cards, advertising and book illustration and has produced two books of his own, *Golf Widows* and *Cricket Widows* (his wife reckons the next one will be *Cartooning Widows!*). He is married and has one daughter, a demented golden retriever and two rabbits.

STANLEY FRANKLIN b1930

Stanley Franklin was born in London and studied drawing at the Hammersmith School of Arts. In 1959 he became political cartoonist of the *Daily Mirror* and left in 1970 to work for television. He has been political cartoonist of the *Sun* since 1974.

NICHOLAS GARLAND b1935

Nicholas Garland was educated partly in New Zealand and studied Fine Art at the Slade School of Art in London. After working in the theatre for some years as stage manager and director he became political cartoonist on the *Daily Telegraph* (1966–86) and has also worked for the *Spectator*, *New Stateman* and *Private Eye*. He is now political cartoonist of the *Independent*.

LES GIBBARD

Les Gibbard was born in New Zealand and became a newspaper reporter at the age of 16. Upon arrival in England he began to specialize in cartooning, initially as arts caricaturist for the *Sunday Telegraph*. He has also worked as an animator for Richard Williams' studio and produced a series of political cartoons for Granada TV and sequences for Channel 4's 'A Week in Politics'. Now 43, Les Gibbard is political cartoonist of the *Guardian* (since 1969) and BBC TV's 'On the Record' programme. He is married, with two Irish wolfhounds, a black labrador and nine cats.

ALEX GRAHAM

A Scot from Dumfries, Alex Graham was educated at Dumfries Academy and Glasgow School of Art and has been a full-time cartoonist since 1945. He is perhaps best known for the 'Fred Basset' strip in the *Daily Mail* which, since it began in 1963, has been syndicated worldwide and been made into twenty TV shorts. His work has also appeared in all the leading British magazines as well as the *New Yorker*. He is married with a grown-up son and daughter and lives in Sussex beside a lake, where he plays golf and bridge and enjoys gardening. He has a Basset hound and a Yorkshire terrier.

DAVID HALDANE

Lives in the north-east of England and is 35 years old. He has been a freelance cartoonist for twelve years, contributing work to *Punch*, *Guardian*, *Daily Mail*, *Spectator*, *Listener*, *Private Eye* and the *Daily Mirror*, and has done some scriptwriting for 'Spitting Image'.

HARRY HARGREAVES

Born in Manchester, Harry Hargreaves studied engineering before serving with RAF Signals in the Far East during the Second World War. Since then he has been a film animator (Disney-trained) and an internationally syndicated free-lance cartoonist and illustrator working in tele-vision, advertising etc. His interests include dogs, birds, cricket, anthropology, conservation, the countryside, the Wildfowl Trust and the Army Air Corps. He is married with two daughters and lives in Somerset.

DAVID HAWKER

Sold his first cartoon in 1967 when working as an architectural draughtsman and went full-time two years later, selling his first cartoon to *Punch* in 1970. He stopped cartooning briefly in 1976 to qualify as a driving instructor and still puts in some part-time hours behind the wheel. Though his work appears in various publications he mainly concentrates on *Punch*.

MARTIN HONEYSETT b1943

Left Croydon School of Art after one year to take to the road. Spent six years abroad in various jobs — as a lumberjack and trucker in Canada — before returning to England in 1969. Began cartooning on his return whilst working as a bus driver for London Transport. Now a full-time cartoonist, appearing mainly in *Private Eye* and *Punch*.

TONY HUSBAND b1950

Had no formal training as an artist but influenced by his father who dabbled in drawing and writing. Found work in the printing side of an advertising agency, as well as spells of window dressing and repairing jewellery. Six and a half years ago his first book of drawings, *Use Your Head*, was pub-lished, and he is now a regular contributor to *Private Eye* and *Punch*. He has won the Cartoonists' Club of Great Britain Joke Cartoonist of the Year award four times and was voted Strip Cartoonist of the Year in 1987. He has also co-written a children's TV programme, *Round the Bend*, for ITV.

'JAC' – JON CARELESS

Corporal Jon Careless enlisted in the Parachute Regiment in 1973 and has served 16 years with the 1st Battalion. He has recently produced, with Sergeant Mawdsley, the *Parachute Regiment Military Cartoon Book*.

IAN JACKSON b1964

Studied at Jacob Kramer College of Art, Leeds, and has been designing greetings cards since 1982 and cartooning regularly for *Punch* since 1984. He also works trotter-in-glove with Uncle Pigg for *Oink!* and occasionally draws cartoons for *Playboy*. When he is not doing any of the above he stuffs animals.

TIMOTHY JAQUES

Educated at Uppingham School, Timothy Jaques received a National Diploma in Design from the London School of Printing in 1957 and was a director of the Peter Hatch Partnership before becoming a freelance graphic designer in 1965. He is consultant designer to a number of com-panies including Nordic Bank, Longman, British Museum Publications and INSEAD Fontaine-bleau, has illustrated books by Jilly Cooper, Arthur Marshall, Douglas Sutherland and Gyles Brandreth amongst others, and has been a fre-quent contributor of cartoons to *Publishing News*.

GRAY JOLLIFFE

After National Service in the RAF, Gray Jolliffe started his career in advertising, working at CDP, DDB, BMP (initially) as a copywriter and became creative director (part-time) of both Chetwynds and Dewe Rogerson. He also tried his hand at directing commercials but packed it in after realiz-ing that he couldn't direct traffic up a one-way street. He was always a cartoonist but until recently no one else knew that. He now does books — notably *Wicked Willie*, which is a world-wide bestseller — and is currently working on a series of children's books featuring the 'Easy Peasy People'. He has a wife and three children, all of whom are nearly as old as he is.

'LARRY' – TERENCE PARKS b1927

'Larry' has been a freelance artist since 1957, contributing mainly to *Punch* and *Private Eye*. For a few 'mad years' in the early 1970s he painted scenery for Joan Littlewood's Theatre Royal in

London. Currently living in Stratford-on-Avon with his wife, 'Larry' has a grown-up son and daughter. He is a great country lover, particularly of the pubs therein, for which he advocates the return of old lino, fag-ends and dogs, and the removal of pile carpets, flower arrangements and canned music.

'MAC' – STAN McMURTRY

'MAC' attended Birmingham College of Art and was a cartoon film animator at Henley-on-Thames before becoming Social and Political Cartoonist of the *Daily Sketch*, later taken over by the *Daily Mail* for whom he has worked ever since. He has been voted Cartoonist of the Year (twice) and Political and Social Cartoonist of the Year by the Cartoonists' Club of Great Britain.

PETER MADDOCKS b1928

Was once told by a psychiatrist that he was 'a creative psychopath'. Boredom with drawing daffodils at Moseley School of Art led him to take off around the world. Returning at the age of 21, he set up his own advertising agency, designing cinema posters, moving on to produce his first cartoons for Fleet Street with the *Daily Sketch*. After periods with the *Daily Express*, *Standard* and *Evening News*, Maddocks went free-lance. Not content with producing animated films for TV, he is also 'headmaster' of the London School of Cartooning.

'MIDI' – MIKE DICKINSON b1938

Mike Dickinson joined the book trade on leaving school and for twenty-five years was a pub-lisher's representative before trying to earn a living in Grub Street. His cartoons first appeared in *Publishing News* in 1982 and he is now a regular weekly contributor. He has also written and illustrated several picture books for children.

'NAM' – NICOLAS MAWDSLEY

Sergeant Nicolas Mawdsley joined the Parachute Regiment in 1968 as a musician and after serving 17 years with the 1st Battalion was posted to Depot Para as Office Manager of the Pegasus Press. He has been the 1st Battalion cartoonist for 17 years.

ROY NIXON b1933

Roy Nixon was born in London but has lived in Chelmsford since 1961. A self-taught artist, he has worked freelance since 1956 (full-time from 1970) for such magazines as *Punch, Private Eye* etc, as well as various national newspapers and overseas publications. He is married with two sons and a daughter.

ROY RAYMONDE

Roy Raymonde attended Harrow School of Art and was much influenced by one of his teachers, Gerard Hoffnung. He became a full-time cartoon-ist and humorist around 1960 and has since gained an international reputation as a regular contributor to *Punch, Playboy* and a variety of other publications worldwide. He is married with two children and lives in Essex.

ARTHUR REID

Arthur Reid has been an international freelance cartoonist, illustrator and sculptor for fifteen years. A graduate of Aberdeen College of Com-merce, Gray's School of Art and Aberdeen Col-lege of Education, he has had work published in *Playboy, Penthouse, Punch* and *Private Eye* and is a part-time art specialist for Grampian Regional Council. His work has also been exhibited world-wide and he has won a number of awards including being the first-ever British Prize Winner of the World Cartoon Exhibition in Belgium in 1980. Arthur Reid is the organizer of the Edinburgh International Cartoon Festival and lists his hobbies as beer and collecting 'first edition' rejection slips. He lives, and sometimes works, in Scotland.

MANDY SHEPHERD

Mandy Shepherd is the daughter of the painter and conservationist, David Shepherd OBE, and has herself been a professional artist for 10 years, concentrating on birds and animals, includ-ing horses and African wildlife. She has travelled widely in Africa and has had a number of one-man shows in Zimbabwe and England. Aged 28, she is married to a surgeon and lives with her husband and daughter near Chichester.

BILL STOTT b1944

Bill Stott was born in Preston, and studied painting and lithography at Harris College in his home town. His greatest influence has been Bill Tidy, and he carries a kidney donor card. He has also recently given up smoking and yearns to write an autobiography as cool as Clive Collins'.

GORDON STOWELL

Gordon Stowell has worked as a freelance designer, illustrator and cartoonist for over thirty years. Much of his work has been for children's books, some of which he has written himself. Cartooning is his first love and he has drawn for a number of national magazines and publishers.

GEOFF THOMPSON

Geoff Thompson is 34 and is married with three children. He works and sleeps in the bedroom of his thatched cottage near Yeovil. A redundancy casualty of the Westland affair, he took to professional cartooning in the autumn of 1986. His drawings have appeared in *Private Eye, Punch, Spectator* and *UK Press Gazette* amongst others.

BILL TIDY b1933

Born in Cheshire, Bill Tidy moved to Liverpool for the Blitz and survived, leaving school at 15 to work in a shipping office. He served with the Royal Engineers from 1952 to 1956 and sold his first cartoon to a Japanese newspaper in 1955. After work in an advertising agency he became a professional cartoonist in 1957 and has regularly contributed to *Punch, Private Eye* and the *Mail on Sunday* among other publications. Perhaps best known for such strips as 'The Cloggies', 'The Fosdyke Saga' and 'The Last Chip Shop in England', Bill Tidy also appears frequently on TV and radio humour shows and has designed stage sets, trophies and ventriloquists' dummies. He is married with two sons and a daughter and lives in the East Midlands.

JOHN TURNER

Since receiving a personally addressed 'Fougasse' cartoon at the age of 10, John Turner has maintained a consuming interest in this form of art. After National Service in the Royal Navy he worked in commercial banking, the motor trade and as a publican and has had cartoons published in *The Universe*, regional newspapers, books and advertising campaigns. He is currently working on a collection of cricket cartoons.

KEITH WAITE

Keith Waite joined Kemsley Newspapers from his native New Zealand in 1951. In the 1950s he worked principally for *Punch* and the *Daily Sketch*, then for a few decades as the editorial cartoonist for the *Daily Mirror* and *Sunday Mirror*. Now in somewhat clapped-out condition he does smaller drawings for *The Times*.

COLIN WHITTOCK b1940

Born in Birmingham, Colin Whittock failed 'O'-level Art and worked in shopfitting until 1979, since when he has been a full-time freelance and has managed to feed his wife, three children and a dog. He now lives in Streetly with a studio in the 'exciting new' Brum centre. Colin Whittock is daily cartoonist for the *Birmingham Evening Mail* and a regular contributor to *Punch*. He is also author/illustrator of the 'Perils of . . .' series of books.

MIKE WILLIAMS b1940

Worked as an illustrator in a commercial art studio before becoming a freelance; now a regular contributor to *Punch, Private Eye* and *Playboy*.

Note Biographical details of other contributors have been omitted at their own request (Ed).

Battle Honours
of the
Parachute Regiment

Regimental motto: *Utrinque paratus* (Ready for Anything)

Arnhem 1944
Athens
Breville
Bruneval
Dives Crossing
Djebel Alliliga
Djebel Azzag 1943
Djebel Dahra
El Hadjeba
Falkland Islands 1982
Goose Green
Greece
Italy 1943–4
Kef el Debna
La Touques Crossing
Merville Battery
Mount Longdon
Normandy Landings
North Africa 1942–3
Northern Europe 1942, 1944–5
Orsogna
Oudna
Ourthe
Pegasus Bridge
Primosole Bridge
Rhine
Sicily
Soudia
Southern France
Tamera
Taranto
Wireless Ridge

(Those in italics are borne
on the Colours)

THE AIRBORNE FORCES CHARITIES DEVELOPMENT TRUST

PATRON: His Royal Highness The Prince of Wales KG KT GCB AK QSO ADC

The Trust has been formed to serve the needs of the five main Airborne Forces charities, which include the Parachute Regimental Fund, the Regimental Association and the museums in Aldershot and Normandy. But the main charity is for those men and their dependants who are in need or distress – The Airborne Forces Security Fund.

Since its inception in 1941, on the initiative of the then Commander British Airborne Forces the late Lieutenant General Sir Frederick Browning, the Airborne Forces Security Fund has disbursed over £3 million in caring for the disabled and the dependants of the 30% casualties suffered by The Parachute Regiment, The Special Air Service Regiment and other units of Airborne Forces in some of the fiercest fighting of the Second World War. Tunisia, Sicily, Italy, Normandy, Arnhem, the Ardennes, the Rhine Crossing, Greece – in these battles the wearers of the Red Beret enhanced the reputation of British Arms, but at great cost.

In the post-war years too, units of Airborne Forces have seen action in various parts of the world; in Egypt, Palestine, Malaysia, Cyprus, Radfan, Aden, Borneo, the Falkland Islands and Northern Ireland. These commitments have resulted in big demands on the Fund's resources. Even in peacetime, training and parachuting involves considerable risk and, regrettably, every year sees more casualties.

Although it is said that the Welfare State provides the essentials of life, only voluntary charitable funds – not bound by regulations and precedents – can give prompt extra help to those Airborne men and their dependants who are in need or distress. In particular there is a very great need for the large number who fought in the Second World War who are now in their seventies and eighties.

For further details contact:

Colonel David Mallam OBE, Regimental Headquarters, The Parachute Regiment, Browning Barracks, Aldershot, Hampshire, GU11 2BU
Aldershot (0252) 316104

THE
DAVID SHEPHERD
CONSERVATION FOUNDATION

For Wildlife and the Environment

PATRON: His Royal Highness Prince Michael of Kent

David asks us all to 'stop and think'.

'Does it really matter if there are no more rhinos left? Does it really matter if, by the end of this century, we will have succeeded in destroying almost all the tropical rain forests of the world? Time is running out for countless species. It's their world too. We all form a part of this intricate and priceless web of life. If we continue to destroy the trees, wildlife and the habitat, man will ultimately destroy himself!

Supporting The David Shepherd Conservation Foundation is one of the ways that you can help. The Foundation supports and complements other wildlife and conservation charities associated with the conservation of the atmosphere, natural habitat, forests, rivers, seas and countryside and their wildlife. It also aids anti-poaching activities in Africa and elsewhere and is actively concerned to halt the misuse of dangerous chemicals and pesticides.

Funds raised in the UK so far have been donated to the Royal Society for Nature Conservation, County Nature Trusts, the Worldwide Fund for Nature, the Young Peoples' Trust for Endangered Species, the International Union for Conservation of Nature, Arts for the Earth, the Men of the Trees, The Woodland Trust, the Whale and Dolphin Conservation Society, the Nigerian Conservation Foundation, The Wildlife Hospital Trust, the European Rhino Walk, UK and US university conservation expeditions in West Africa and Thailand, Voluntary Service Overseas' conservation projects, and a number of other anti-poaching and wildlife-protection measures.

Charity Regd No: 289646

For further details contact:

Michael Zilka, The Administrator, The David Shepherd Conservation Foundation,
PO Box 123, Godalming, Surrey GU8 4JS
Hascombe (048632) 576/220